Object Talks

for Special Days

STANDARD PUBLISHING
Cincinnati, Ohio   2859

Illustrated by Richard Briggs

ISBN: 0-87239-723-8

Contents

Talks for Special Days

Communion, Invitation, and Stewardship Talks

Talks for
Special Days

Forming Good Habits

(New Year's Day)

> . . . blessed are those who keep my ways.
> —*Proverbs 8:32*

Objects Needed: Two calendars, one of the old year and one of the new year; marker; wastebasket

This is the beginning of a new year. Last year's calendars are no longer useful to us, so we throw them away and use the calendars for the new year just beginning. As we throw away our old calendars, let's try to throw away all our bad habits. Who can name some bad habits that we need to get rid of? (As the children name the bad habits, list them on the old calendar so the children can see them. Read over the list aloud when you're done, then throw it in the wastebasket.)

But throwing away our bad habits is not enough. As we throw them away we must form good habits and make them an important part of our daily lives. What are some good habits we ought to have? (List these in the new calendar, or on a sheet of paper to be attached to the calendar later.)

Let's begin this new year determined to try harder to develop good habits. That way, we can be a blessing to our homes and our Savior.

—*Idalee Vonk*

Four Kinds of Hearts

(New Year's Day)

> But what was sown on good soil is the man who hears the word and understands it.
> —*Matthew 13:23*

Objects Needed: Four colored paper hearts; black, gray, brown, and red

How many of you know where your heart is? Where is it? (Let the children point to their chests.) What does your heart do? (Pumps blood.)

That's right. But did you know that you have another heart? You do, and it doesn't pump any blood at all. This is the heart that is mentioned in the Bible a lot by Jesus. It is the part of us that controls all our thoughts and feelings, but no one can see it or touch it. We might call it our "spiritual heart."

Jesus tells us that there are four kinds of these "spiritual hearts" that people can have. Each one of these hearts reacts differently when it hears the Word of God.

(Show the black heart.) The first is a stony heart that does not pay attention to God's Word and really is not interested in learning what God has to say.

(Show the gray heart.) The second is a very shallow heart that listens to God's Word at first, but then forgets all about it when it becomes difficult to live up to what God says.

(Show the brown heart.) The third heart is a pleasure-seeking heart. It enjoys money and the good things it can buy so much that it would rather have fun all the time instead of paying attention to God and what He wants.

(Show the red heart.) The fourth kind of heart is a good heart. It listens to God's Word and then tries its best to understand what God is saying and to live accordingly.

8

This is the kind of heart God wants us to have, and if we ask Him for it He will give it to us. If you don't think you have this kind of heart, why not ask God to give you one? Wouldn't it be great to start a new year with a new heart?

—*Duane Kellogg*

Show Love to Others

(Valentine's Day)

As I have loved you, so you must love one another. All men will know that you are my disciples if you love one another.

—*John 13:34, 35*

Object Needed: A Valentine card

Do any of you know of a special day that will be coming up this week? That's right, it will be Valentine's Day soon, and maybe you'll be getting Valentine cards like this one that I brought with me this morning. How many of you will be giving Valentine cards to other people? That's good, because as Christians we are supposed to love other people, and Valentine cards are a way of telling other people that we *do* love them.

When I was in school, there was a boy in my class that nobody seemed to like. On Valentine's Day he would feel very sad because nobody wanted to give him a Valentine. I was afraid to send him one because the other kids might find out and start laughing at me. But do you think that was right? Of course not. As Christians we're supposed to love everyone, even those people that no one else seems to like.

I know it may be hard to do, but if you want to please God, why not send a Valentine to someone other people

don't like or make fun of, and then try to be his friend. This will show that your faith in Jesus is real, not just make-believe. Stand up for Jesus by doing what will please Him, and don't worry about what the other children might say.
—*Duane Kellogg*

Jesus Was Misunderstood

(Palm Sunday)

The great crowd . . . took palm branches and went out to meet him, shouting, "Hosanna! . . . Blessed is the King of Israel!"
—*John 12:12, 13*

Object Needed: A palm leaf or branch

If Jesus were to ride into town today, do you think He would ride in a military tank or a Volkswagen 'bug'? (Let them respond.) Jesus was a humble man of peace, not a man of war. I think He would probably ride in a VW.

If you were to greet Him when He came by, would you take an American flag or would you take a Christian flag? (Show them a Christian flag if you have one.) Jesus is not just a national or political hero. He is the Prince of Peace and He reigns over the whole world as our Lord, so a Christian flag would be more appropriate to wave for Jesus.

But now look at this palm leaf. You remember when Jesus rode into Jerusalem just before He was crucified. He rode not on a majestic stallion or in a spectacular war chariot, but on a humble little donkey. Nevertheless, the people greeted Him like they would a military hero. Back then, palm branches were the national symbol of Palestine and were waved like we might wave little American flags today.

By doing that, the people showed that they really did not

10

understand who Jesus was nor why He had come. They either did not know or did not understand the Scripture verses that would have told them these things. If they had known and understood the Bible better, they would not have made such a mistake. And that is why it is important for us to know and understand the Bible, because it is there that we come to know and understand who Jesus really is—the Son of God who came to die for our sins, that we might be able to go to Heaven.

So keep reading and studying the Bible and learn all you can about it, and then try to interest your friends and family in reading it too. That way they can greet Jesus and receive Him into their lives.

—*Duane Kellogg*

Stronger Than Death

(Good Friday)

Thanks be to God! He gives us the victory through our Lord Jesus Christ.
— *1 Corinthians 15:57*

Object Needed: Something that looks frightening, but is actually harmless; e.g. a rubber snake

(Open the bag and pretend you are trying to grab a real snake inside it.) How many of you like snakes? (Pull the snake out quickly and hold it close to one of the children while wiggling it around.)

Many people are afraid of snakes because some of them carry a deadly poison in their fangs. If a poisonous snake were to bite you, it would hurt very much, and it could even kill you.

11

When I first took this rubber snake out of the bag, it may have frightened you because you thought it was real. But now that you know it is just rubber you realize that there is nothing to be frightened about. It certainly can't hurt you.

That's what the Bible tells us death is like for Christians. It may look frightening at first, but it really can't harm us. There is no reason for Christians to be afraid of death. And do you know why? Because Jesus has removed death's fangs. By dying on the cross and rising from the dead, Jesus has opened the way for all of us who are His followers to rise from the dead as well.

That means that when we die, we merely enter into a new and better life with Jesus where we will know happiness and laughter forever. That is why we celebrate Jesus' resurrection on Easter. Because He defeated death by coming to life again, we who are Christians need fear death no longer. It is as harmless as this rubber snake.

—*Duane Kellogg*

The Proof About Jesus

(Easter)

But these are written that you may believe that Jesus is the Christ, the Son of God, and that by believing you may have life in his name.   *—John 20:31*

Object Needed: Something with an official seal on it, like a diploma

Can any of you tell me what is on the diploma I have? Take a good look at it. What do you suppose it could be? (Let them guess.) It is an official seal. Let me show you how it works (press a piece of paper in the seal and show them the imprint)

A seal like this is used on important documents to confirm that they are authentic and true. In a way, a seal guarantees that what is said on that piece of paper is true, and that it was not forged or copied by someone who might be trying to deceive and trick people who read it.

In a way, that is what the resurrection of Jesus is like. It is like a seal that guarantees that Jesus really was who He said He was—the Messiah, the Son of God. The resurrection proves that Jesus was not a phony, that He was not trying to trick people, but that everything He said was true.

If Jesus was just a great and very wise man, He would have remained in the tomb like all the great and wise men before Him. But He was not just a great man. He was and is God, and His resurrection proves it.

So if you and I really believe that Jesus rose from the dead, we will want to follow and obey Jesus and worship Him as our God. If we do, then we will be given the gift of eternal life, and someday we too will be raised from the dead and live forever, just like Jesus.

—Duane Kellogg

13

The Empty Tomb

(Easter)

"Why do you look for the living among the dead? He is not here; he has risen!"
—Luke 24:5, 6

Object Needed: An empty jar

Today is a very special day. Who can tell me why? Why are we happy on Easter Sunday? (Let them give various answers until someone mentions Jesus' resurrection, then hold up the empty jar.) Can anyone tell me what kind of jar this is?

In a way, Easter is a very strange holiday. On this holiday we celebrate because something was empty! Now isn't that strange? Usually we are happy because something is full— not empty. We are happy because we have a bag *full* of candy. We are happy because we have a piggy bank *full* of money. We are happy because we have a refrigerator *full* of good food.

How many of you are happy to see this empty jar? It's not really anything to get excited about, is it? You'd be much happier to see it if it was full of candy, wouldn't you?

But like I said before, on Easter we celebrate because something was empty. Do any of you know what was empty? (The tomb where they laid Jesus' dead body.) And do you know why we are so happy about an empty tomb? (It means that Jesus rose from the dead.) And do you know what that means for us? It means that if we follow Jesus as our Lord and Savior in this life, we will also follow Him when we die. We will be given new bodies in Heaven, bodies that will never get old, or sick, or hurt. And we will live with Jesus forever.

That is *good news!* And that is why we are so happy over something that was empty. —*Duane Kellogg*

God Cares for Us

(Mother's Day)

"O Jerusalem, . . . how often I have longed to gather your children together, as a hen gathers her chicks under her wings. . . ."
— *Matthew 23:37*

Objects Needed: Baby bottle, blanket, map or compass, paper heart

I'll bet all of you know what special day it is today. That's right, it is Mother's Day. Mothers do an awful lot for us. I brought some things with me this morning to remind us of just some of the things mothers do for us.

First, I have this baby bottle. This reminds us that mothers feed us and nurture us when we are little so that we will grow up big and strong.

Next, I have a blanket. What do you suppose this should remind us of? (Let them share their ideas.) It reminds us how mothers make us feel warm and secure and comfort us when we are hurt or just tired.

Third, I have a compass with me. Have any of you ever used a compass? Do you know what a compass is used for? It helps us tell what direction we are going. Mothers do that for us too—they teach us and train us and guide us to go in the right direction.

And finally, I have this big red heart. What do you suppose that stands for? Love, that's right. A mother gives her love and warmth and lets us know she cares about us.

These are all very important things that mothers do. And did you know that if you are a Christian, God takes care of you in many ways just like a mother does? That's right. We often speak about God as our heavenly Father, but in some ways He acts as our mother, too. Like a mother, God's Spirit feeds and nurtures us, comforts us when we hurt, guides and teaches us as we read the Bible, and loves us in a warm and personal way.

I hope you have experienced this in your own life so that you can celebrate Mother's Day for two reasons—one for the wonderful gift of your human mother and the other for the matchless gift of God's loving care.

—*Duane Kellogg*

Building on the Past

(Memorial Day)

Remember the words I spoke to you.
—*John 15:20*

Objects Needed: A page from a coloring book, a blank page, and some crayons

If someone were to ask me to draw a picture of a man standing on his head or a fish in a fishtank, I could try (do so on the blank page), but it wouldn't come out very well. But if I were given the outline of the picture, like in this coloring book, I could easily finish it by filling in the colors.

This week we will be celebrating Memorial Day. It is a day when we think back with thankfulness for the good things done by people who lived before us. Because of their hard work, we have been given a lot of help in doing our work today. In a sense, they have drawn us the outline, and all we have to do is fill in the colors. We don't have to start from scratch.

One of the things we have been given is this church. Another thing we have been given to go along with it is the freedom to worship and share our faith with others. A lot of people in this world do not enjoy such freedom. For these and many other things we can be grateful.

But how are we making the church more beautiful and more colorful? Are we adding anything to what we have been given by filling in the outlines? I hope each of us will

16

try to make full use of what we have been given and find ways to make our church even better.

—*Duane Kellogg*

God Sends His Spirit

(Pentecost)

> You, however, are not controlled by the sinful nature but by the Spirit, if the Spirit of God lives in you. —*Romans 8:9*

Object Needed: A fan

I brought a little fan with me this morning, and I want someone to tell me if they can see the wind that it makes (waves the fan in the air a few times). Nobody? Okay, now I want to know if you can *feel* the wind the fan makes (wave the fan near someone's face). You can? Now I want you to tell me if you can see the wind move something (fan someone's hair or a little piece of paper).

We can *feel* the wind and we can *see* what it does, but we can't actually see the wind itself, can we?

Well, the same thing is true of God the Holy Spirit. After Jesus rose from the dead and went back to Heaven, He sent His Holy Spirit into the world to take His place. If it helps, you might think of Jesus being like this fan who continues to send His Spirit, which we can't see, into the world.

But even though we can't *see* the Holy Spirit, when He comes into our lives we can *feel* Him and we can see the effect He has on us and on others.

Today we celebrate the anniversary of the Holy Spirit being sent into the world, to be with us and to live in every Christian. We call today Pentecost Sunday. Just like Easter, it is a very important and happy day in the life of the church.

—*Duane Kellogg*

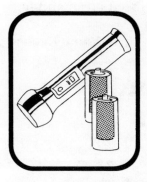

The Power of the Holy Spirit

(Pentecost)

I will pour out my Spirit on all people.
—Acts 2:17

Object Needed: A flashlight, with the batteries taken out

I brought a flashlight with me this morning and I'm going to turn it on right now (flip the switch on). Hey, what's the matter? There's no light coming on. I'm sure all the parts are here. What do you think is the problem with it?

Maybe we'd better check the batteries (open it up and look inside). Oh, there aren't any in it! No wonder it didn't work. It's a good thing I just happened to have one in my pocket (put in one battery). Hey, it still doesn't work. Maybe it needs another battery (put in the other battery). There it goes. Now we have some light.

We are a lot like this flashlight. Just like the flashlight needs to be filled with two batteries in order for it to work, so we too need to be filled with the Holy Spirit in order to live as Christians and let our light shine before men.

Today is a very important day for the church. It's the day we celebrate the giving of the Holy Spirit to all believers in Christ. We call it Pentecost Sunday. When we become Christians, the Holy Spirit comes and lives inside us and gives us the power we need to follow Jesus.

But we need to have our power source recharged regularly or it gets drained out, just like a battery. The way we get our power recharged is by staying in contact with God through prayer, reading the Bible, and going to church and Sunday school. If we remember to do these things then our power source, the Holy Spirit, will always be at full strength within us, and our light will be bright and clear.

—Duane Kellogg

Flashlight bulb
Battery with wire connected
to each terminal.

Paper, pencil & tape

Jesus, Our Standard

(Father's Day)

Be imitators of God, therefore, as dearly loved children and live a life of love, just as Christ loved us . . .   —*Ephesians 5:1, 2*

Objects Needed: A twelve-inch ruler; six strips of paper, each slightly shorter than the one before.

I brought a ruler with me this morning. As you can see, it is exactly twelve inches long. Now, I wanted to cut several strips of paper so that they would all be twelve inches long. But do you know what I did? I measured the first piece with the ruler and cut it as you can see. It is almost exactly twelve inches long (hold it up next to the ruler). So, instead of using the ruler again, I used this piece of paper to measure the next one. As you can see, it is pretty close (hold up the first and second strips of paper to compare them). I then used this second piece of paper to measure the next one, and the next one to measure the next one until I had all six pieces of paper that I wanted.

The only trouble is, look how far off this last piece is from the twelve-inch ruler (hold the sixth piece up next to the ruler). It's over a quarter of an inch shorter! That is not very good. I would have been much smarter if I used the ruler to measure each strip of paper, so that this last piece would be at least as close to the twelve inches as the first one that I cut. It is always better to stick with the original thing you are using to measure with.

As you know, today is Father's Day. Many of us don't realize all the responsibilities our fathers have on their shoulders. One of the most important duties of a Christian father is to show his children how they should live by being a good example for them. But do you know who fathers are supposed to follow so that *they* know how to live right? (Jesus) That's right, it's Jesus. We might think of Jesus as being like this ruler. Fathers are supposed to look to him in order to guide and measure their lives.

But fathers are human and fathers make mistakes.

Sometimes fathers come up a little short when measured against Jesus. So if we only look to our fathers as models of how to live, we can only come as close to Jesus as they are.

Let your fathers show you the best they know how to live, and then push off from there and try to get even closer to the way Jesus lived than your father did. i'm sure every one of your fathers would be happy and proud to see you do this, because they know that the closer we come to measuring up to Jesus' example, the better off we will be.

—*Duane Kellogg*

That's Big!

(for camp or outdoors)

When I consider your heavens, the work of your fingers, the moon and stars, which you have set in place, what is man, that you are mindful of him? —*Psalm 8:3, 4*

Object Needed: A book of astronomy with pictures, or a clear night sky

The universe is the whole of everything that exists. Although astronomers have studied and learned much about the universe, it is so large and mysterious that there is much we still do not understand about it.

What we do know is that space is endless and empty. It contains no water or air. It surrounds stars, planets, moons, comets, asteroids, and meteors.

The sun is a star that shines brightly because of nuclear energy. At its center the heat of its energy reaches twenty-seven million degrees.

The earth travels around the sun at sixty-six thousand miles per hour. While it circles the sun it is also spinning, like a top, at a high rate of speed.

A galaxy is a group of stars. There are one hundred fifty billion stars in our galaxy, and astronomers believe there are billions of galaxies in space.

Distances in space are so vast that they can't be measured in miles. Instead they are measured in light-years. A light-year is the amount of distance light can travel in one year. One light-year equals 5.88 trillion miles!

All of these facts seem beyond our understanding. It's difficult even to think about something so large, powerful, and wondrous.

When we look into the sky on a dark, starry night we can only guess about what is out there and how it all works, but one thing we know for sure: the universe is controlled by God! All the power, wonder, and size are part of His plan.

You are a part of this wonderful universe. Let God control your life. He has the understanding and power to do so.

—*Lois Edstrom*

Do Everything for the Lord

(Labor Day Sunday)

Whatever you do, whether in word or deed, do it all in the name of the Lord Jesus . . .
—*Colossians 3:17*

Objects Needed: A Bible; tools or supplies representing various professions.

I brought a lot of different items with me this morning, as you can see (lay all the objects out where they can see them). What I would like to know is which one of these things would you pick if you were going to do the Lord's work? (They will probably choose the Bible.) That's very interesting. You're right of course—the Bible would be a very good thing to have if you were doing the Lord's work.

But did you know that when we become Christians everything we do should be the Lord's work? A Christian who builds houses is doing the Lord's work (hold up hammer). A Christian who fixes cars or plumbing is doing the Lord's work (hold up wrench). A person who plants a garden is doing the Lord's work (hold up trowel). A Christian who works in an office, or teaches school, or goes to school and studies is doing the Lord's work (hold up pencil). A Christian who cuts the grass is doing the Lord's work (hold up grass shears). A Christian who takes care of a home and cleans windows is doing the Lord's work.

Once we become Christians, everything we do should be done for the Lord. And that's why we should always try to do our best because we are working for God. Try to keep this in mind when you go back to school. When you do your schoolwork, you are working for Jesus. So always try to do your best, because as a Christian you bear the name of Christ.

—*Duane Kellogg*

Giving Thanks

(Thanksgiving Sunday)

Enter his gates with thanksgiving . . . for the
Lord is good. —Psalm 100:4, 5

Object Needed: A patchwork quilt, any size

When we look at this quilt, the first things that catch our
eyes are the many brightly colored patches. Just glancing
at the quilt, we see many patches and many colors, but if
we take time to look at the whole quilt very carefully, we
would find more and more patches and more and more
colors.

This patchwork quilt is like our lives. The patches are
like the blessings God gives to us each day. When we think
of God's blessings, we always think of certain ones first—
like clothing, food, our homes, our parents, our brothers
and sisters, our friends, schools, churches, the Bible, and
the greatest of all blessings, Jesus, our Lord and Savior.

The longer we look at this quilt the more patches we see.
The longer we look at our lives the more blessings we find—
health, the blessings of sight, speech, and hearing, healthy
bodies, the sun, rain, wind, trees, flowers, animals, pets,
the seasons, books, toys, bikes. We could go on and on
listing blessings, for our lives are so full of them.

If we tried to count every piece on this quilt, it would take
us a long time. It surely would take us a long, long time to
count every blessing God has given to us. The bigger the
quilt, the more pieces. The older we grow, the more blessings we shall receive. We should give thanks to God each
day for them.

—Idalee Vonk

23

Appreciation

(Thanksgiving Sunday)

Give thanks in all circumstances, for this is God's will for you in Christ Jesus.
— *1 Thessalonians 5:18*

Object Needed: A magazine that contains many colorful pictures

This magazine is filled with beautiful, colored pictures. If I turn the pages slowly, one by one, you have time to see the beauty of each page. You an see all the details and appreciate the pictures and the beautiful colors.

The faster I turn the pages the less time you have to see the pictures. Much of the beauty and the detail are lost. If I hold the magazine in one hand and just run my thumb along the edge of the pages like this, you won't see anything clearly. Everything will look blurred.

When we take time to appreciate the things given to us, it's like turning the pages of a magazine slowly, one page at a time. Appreciating something given to us or done for us means more than just saying thanks. It means looking at the gift carefully so we can enjoy all its beauty. It means using the gift in the right way and taking good care of it.

But when we don't appreciate the things people do for us, it's like turning pages of this magazine so fast we can't see the beauty of each picture. And when we take everything given to us for granted without even a word of thanks, it's like running our thumb along the edge of the pages so that everything is just a blur.

In order to receive the most good from a picture, we must study each detail carefully. In order to get the most from what is given to us, we must use the gifts the very best way we can. What are some ways we can show our thanks to God for all the wonderful gifts He gives us?

—*Idalee Vonk*

24

Get Ready for Jesus

(First Sunday in Advent)

. . . Prepare the way for the Lord; make straight in the wilderness a highway for our God.

—Isaiah 40:3

Object Needed: A picture of a piece of mouth-watering cake from a magazine ad.

I was looking through a magazine recently, and I came across this picture of a piece of cake (show them the picture). Doesn't that look delicious? It makes you want a piece, doesn't it? That's the whole purpose behind this advertisement—so you will go out and get some.

But there are a few things you have to do before you can actually sit down and eat some cake like this. First, you need to get some money so you can buy the cake mix. Then you have to go to the store, find it on the shelf, and pay for it at the counter. Then you have to bring it home, mix in the right ingredients, bake it, let it cool, and frost it. Then finally you can cut yourself a piece and eat it. That's a lot of preparation between seeing the cake in a magazine and eating a piece yourself.

In a way the Bible is like this advertisement. It describes how wonderful Jesus is and it talks about His love and kindness. When we read it, it makes us want to have more of Jesus in our lives. But before that can happen, we must do a few things to prepare for this.

That is really what Advent is all about. Advent starts today and ends on Christmas day. It is a time when we should be preparing to celebrate the coming of Jesus into the world. It is also a time to be preparing our hearts and minds to receive Him more fully into our own lives.

Probably the most important thing we who are already Christians can do is to try harder than ever to live like God

25

wants us to, being helpful to our parents and teachers and obeying them. We should also tell God we are sorry for anything we have done wrong and that we will try never to do it again.

If we will do these things, then we will be preparing more room in our lives for Jesus. That means we will be sure to have a merrier Christmas than we have ever had before.

—*Duane Kellogg*

A Special Child

(Christmas)

I bring you good news of great joy that will be for all the people. —*Luke 2:10*

Objects Needed: Baby clothes and supplies

I have brought a box of clothes for you to look at while we talk. Feel how soft they are. Notice that there is a sweater, shirt, nightgown, hat, a pair of slippers, and a blanket. Does anyone in our group have feet that would fit in these slippers? Who would wear clothes like these? Babies!

You were once a baby, and you were so tiny that you were able to wear clothes like these.

When a family is expecting a baby, there is much excitement as the parents make preparations for the new child. They prepare a bed and buy soft, warm clothes.

After a baby is born the family is happy. They want to spread the news and tell everyone about the new child. Often they send out birth announcements to let people know when the baby was born, the name, and the weight of the infant.

Friends come to admire the child. They wonder what the baby will do with his life when he is an adult. That little

26

person may become a farmer, doctor, teacher, scientist, homemaker, or artist. There are many choices.

Many years ago a very special baby was born. His name was Jesus. His mother and father loved Him very much, but because they were poor and had been traveling, they didn't have a bed or clothes for Him. His mother took strips of cloth, called swaddling clothes, and wrapped them around the baby. A box that had held hay for the cattle was used as His bed.

This baby was so special that an angel spread the news of His birth: "I bring you good news of great joy that will be for all the people." The angels sang and a bright star twinkled over the place where He was born. Many people came to admire Him and worship Him. There was great joy because people knew He had been sent from God to be a Savior for all the people of the world.

We still talk about the birth of this special baby because His birth gave hope to everyone. When He was born there were no soft clothes or a crib, but there was love. His purpose was to bring love into the world, and we are still experiencing that love.

This Christmas, when we celebrate the birth of Jesus, think about the hope, joy, and love He gave to the world.

—*Lois Edstrom*

God's Wonderful Gift

(Christmas)

For it is by grace you have been saved, through faith — and this not from yourselves, it is the gift of God. —*Ephesians 2:8*

Object Needed: A Christmas package

How many of you expect to get everything you want on Christmas day? Well, even if you don't, I'm sure you'll get a lot of nice presents.

I brought a Christmas present with me this morning, and I want to show it to you. Now if I want to give this to somebody, what does that person have to do? (Put out their hand to receive it.)

That's right. In order for anyone to give us something, we have to be willing to receive it.

What was God's gift to the world on the first Christmas? That's right, it was Jesus. God's gift of Jesus is offered to anyone who is willing to receive it.

But many people, though they see the gift being offered to them, refuse to receive it for themselves. I hope all of you will receive Jesus Christ into your lives and not just look at Him from a distance. For when you do, you will see that He is the best gift of all.

—*Duane Kellogg*

Communion, Invitation, and Stewardship Talks

Remembering Jesus

Do this in remembrance of me.
—1 Corinthians 11:24

Object Needed: A gravestone made from gray construction paper, with a name and the dates of birth and death

Who can guess what I have here? (Show back of tombstone, which has no writing.) That's right, it's a tombstone (show the inscription on the front). Do you know why we put tombstones on people's graves? (Wait until someone says that it's a way of remembering them.)

Have any of you ever seen a picture of Jesus' tombstone? No? Well, that's because He doesn't have a tombstone on His grave. In fact, He doesn't even *have* a grave. That's because Jesus rose up out of the grave on the third day after He died. Jesus knew that was going to happen, and that is one reason why He asked His followers to begin taking part in what we call the Lord's Supper or Communion. You might say that this (point to Communion table) is Jesus' tombstone. It's one way He gave us to always remember Him.

Christians all over the world celebrate Communion, remembering what Jesus has done for us. Someday I hope all of you will be joining us in this event. Until then, there are other ways we can remember Jesus. One of the best ways is to try to be like Jesus and to do what He tells us to do in the Bible: telling others about Him, sharing with others, helping people who are in trouble or having problems, and being a friend to someone who is lonely. If you do these things, then you will be remembering Jesus in a wonderful way.

—Duane Kellogg

What the Cross Stands For

For the message of the cross is foolishness to those who are perishing, but to us who are being saved it is the power of God.
—1 Corinthians 1:18

Objects Needed: A cross; a rabbit's foot (or some other "lucky" item)

Who can tell me what I have here this morning? (Show them the rabbit's foot.) Do you know why anyone would carry a rabbit's foot around with them? Many people think a rabbit's foot brings them good luck. What are some other things that people say bring good luck? (horseshoe, four-leaf clover) Do you know what we call such ideas? (superstitions) They are just superstitions; they really have no power to affect what happens to us one way or another.

There is another thing people carry around with them sometimes, and they treat this thing just like a rabbit's foot. But it really represents something very powerful that *can* make a real change in our lives. I brought one of these along with me this morning also (show them the cross). As you can see it's a cross. Now really, it is only a piece of wood with a certain shape, and it is of no more value than this rabbit's foot.

What makes a cross like this important is what it *stands* for. It reminds us of the fact that God became a man named Jesus, and died on a cross, and rose from the dead. Because Jesus is no longer dead, but living, we can know God through Him by asking Jesus to share our lives with us and to be our constant guide, companion, and friend.

What a wonderful thing it is to be able to know God personally and to serve Him every day. I hope all of you who don't know Him already will soon come to know Him and to follow Him the rest of your lives.

—*Duane Kellogg*

Communicating With Jesus

A man ought to examine himself before he eats of the bread and drinks of the cup.
—1 Corinthians 11:28

Object Needed: A telephone

I'm sure all of you have used a telephone, haven't you? Well, I brought one with me this morning in order to show you something. Who would you like to call up on this phone? (Let them suggest some people.) There is only one problem though, isn't there? It's not connected!

In order for us to talk with someone else on the phone, certain conditions must be met. First, our phone must be plugged in and working. But now let's pretend this phone is plugged and working. What are some other conditions that must be met before we can talk to someone else on the phone? (You have to dial the right number, other person must have a phone, other person must be home, etc.) So, then, a number of conditions must be met before we can talk with someone else on the phone.

As you can see here before you, we will be celebrating the Lord's Supper. Jesus told us to do this as a way of communicating with Him. In fact, sometimes we call the Lord's Supper "Communion," don't we? But in order to really communicate with God when we participate in the Lord's Supper, certain conditions must be met.

First, we must believe in Jesus Christ and accept Him as our Lord and Savior. Second, we must have the proper attitudes. We must be sorry for our sins, we must be willing to forgive all those who have hurt us, and we must try to live more like the way we know Jesus wants us to live.

When we do all this, then God comes to us in a special way during the Lord's Supper, and gives us added strength and comfort for the days ahead. **—Duane Kellogg**

33

Make This Connection

For there is one God and one mediator between God and men, the man Christ Jesus.
— *1 Timothy 2:5*

Object Needed: A kite (this lesson could be expanded by building a kite)

A windy day is a perfect day to fly a kite. It's great fun to run fast, pulling a kite on the end of a string, and feel it lift into the air. If you unwind more string from its holder, the kite will soar higher into the sky.

The thin pieces of wood or plastic in a kite hold it rigid so its surface can catch the wind. The tail of the kite provides balance.

Perhaps the most important part of a kite is the string. Without the string the kite wouldn't fly. It couldn't get airborne and it wouldn't stay in the air. The string *connects* up to the kite. That line holds the kite steady and gives it *stability*. It holds the kite in the air. If you let go of the line the tension would be broken and the kite would fall to the ground.

When we think about a person flying a kite we can see a picture of how we should place Christ in our lives. Jesus is the lifeline between God and us. When Jesus Christ died on the cross, He made it possible for us to be connected to God.

When we place Jesus Christ in our lives as our *connection* to God, He holds us steady and gives us *stability*. We need to hold tightly to Christ, just as we hold on to a kite string. We are connected to a wonderful God!

—*Lois Edstrom*

34

also see next page

Stay Connected

I can do everything through him who gives me strength. —*Philippians 4:13*

Objects Needed: A flashlight bulb, and a battery with a wire connected to each of its terminals

As you can see, I have a flashlight bulb with me this morning. A bulb like this by itself is not much good for anything. It has to be connected to a power source in order to do what it is supposed to do, which is to give off light.

Can any of you tell me why God created you and me? (Let them respond.) In a general sense, we can say He made us to love Him, to love one another, and to bring Him honor. But we can't do that without God's help. We, like a light bulb, must be hooked up to a power source. We 'hook up' with God when we accept Jesus into our lives as our Lord and Savior. Then we are able to produce light and warmth, like this light bulb does when I touch these wires to its base (do so).

When we do something wrong, it's as if one of our wires becomes disconnected, because God can't stand sin near Him (disconnect one of the wires). Our light and warmth disappear and God seems far away. We are still connected to God, but we don't have His power flowing through us.

If we want to really experience God's power and love in our lives, we must confess our sin to God and tell Him we are sorry. Then we can be reconnected, and experience God's power flowing through us (reconnect the wire).

If God seems far away from you, and you don't feel His presence in your life, it may be because you have done something wrong and have not sought God's forgiveness. You can be certain that if you do so, He will forgive you and you will come to experience God in a more real and personal way.

—*Duane Kellogg*

Jesus Removes Our Sin

We have been made holy through the sacrifice of the body of Jesus Christ once for all.
—*Hebrews 10:10*

Objects Needed: A piece of paper, a pencil, and some tape

How many of you have ever made a sign? What did you make it for? (Let them respond.) I want to make a sign this morning with this piece of paper. I want to let everyone know that Jesus loves us, so that is what I am going to write (do so, only make a mistake—for example, 'Jesus *lives* us'). There, how's that? (Let someone read it out loud).

Jesus *lives* us? Oh, I see I have made a mistake. It was supposed to say 'Jesus loves us.' Well that's easy to fix, I'll just cover it up and write over it (tape a piece of paper over the mistake and correct it). There, now the mistake is gone, isn't it? Well, not really. You and I both know that it is still there underneath this piece of paper. It's just been covered up. Someone would notice this piece of paper taped on here and pull it off and find the mistake I made (do so).

What would be a better way to get rid of this mistake? (Let them answer.) That's right, we could erase it (do so). Then I can easily write the correct letter in its place (do so). Now no one will be able to uncover my mistake because it is gone. I have erased it.

That is what God does with our sin when we tell Him we are sorry and that we will try never to do it again. He doesn't just cover our sins over—He erases them and He forgets about them. He can do that because when we accept Jesus as our Savior, He takes our sins on himself and removes them from us. He then washes them completely away and they are gone forever. We never have to feel guilty about things we did wrong in the past. As far as God is concerned, we are perfect and our sins are forgotten.

So don't worry about something you may have done wrong in the past. If you have told God you are sorry and you will try not to do it again, God has forgotten all about it, and you should try to do the same. —*Duane Kellogg*

The Vine and the Branches

I am the vine; you are the branches. If a man remains in me and I in him, he will bear much fruit; apart from me you can do nothing.
—*John 15:5*

Object Needed: A plant

Jesus once compared himself to a vine. He said His followers were like the branches that grow out from the vine. Since I didn't have a vine I could bring in, I brought in this plant to show you the same thing. We might say that Jesus is like the main part of the plant, and we are like the offshoots (point out the different parts).

Now what happens if I break off one of these offshoots? (Break a piece off.) Will it be able to live on its own? It has to be attached to the main part of the plant, doesn't it?

The same is true with us. We have to be attached to Jesus if we are to grow in our Christian lives, and we have to stay attached. It won't do any good just to attach ourselves to Him once a week when we come to church.

How do we separate ourselves from Jesus? (Unconfessed sin, not putting Jesus first, etc.)

How can we stay close to Jesus during the week? (Prayer, reading the Bible, helping others, etc.)

I hope all of you will remember to stay close to Jesus this week, and every week, so that you will continue to grow into the kind of person God wants you to be.

—*Duane Kellogg*

Cleansing From Sin

Jesus answered, ''A person who has had a bath needs only to wash his feet; his whole body is clean.'' —*John 13:10*

Object Needed: Package of ''Wash & Dri'' or other hand cleaner

When I got up this morning, I took a shower so I would be good and clean to come to church. But that was several hours ago. If I were going to pick up something and eat it with my fingers, I would want to wash my hands again first. Even though they may look clean, they probably have dirt on them that we can't see, just from touching things like books, papers, and the steering wheel of my car. We can't help but come in contact with such things, and that's why it's a good idea to wash our hands just before we eat, even if we did take a shower or a bath in the morning.

So, if I want my hands to be good and clean, I could use something like this (pull out a "Wash & Dri" and wash your hands). Now I can clean them right on the spot.

When we accept Jesus as our Savior and Lord, He makes us more clean than any shower or bath ever could. He removes every speck and particle of sin that clings to us, so we can become pure in God's eyes. This is possible only because Jesus died for us, and only because we accept His salvation for ourselves.

After that happens, it will be impossible for us to avoid getting parts of us dirty again, because we are surrounded by sin and evil. But we never have to be completely bathed by Jesus again. We don't have to accept Him into our lives again and again. Once He comes, He comes to stay.

But we do, as I said, get dirty because of the sins we commit now. When that happens, we need to have our hands washed by admitting our sin, confessing it to God, and asking for His forgiveness. That's like using one of these (hold up "Wash & Dri") to wash our hands. We don't need another complete bath.

So if you have accepted Jesus into your life then you have taken your bath, and you are clean in God's eyes. But when you sin now, you still need to ask for God's forgiveness. And if you confess your sins to Him, He will forgive you and make you clean again. —*Duane Kellogg*

Wanted: Dead and Alive

Set your minds on things above, not on earthly things. For you died, and your life is now hidden with Christ in God.
—*Colossians 3:2, 3*

Object Needed: A mirror, with a caption reading "Wanted: Dead and Alive"

How many of you have ever seen an FBI wanted poster in the post office? They used to make them a little differently a long time ago. You have probably seen a "Wanted: Dead or Alive" poster on a TV western. Well, I brought one with me this morning and I want one person to come up here and tell me who they see on this poster (have an older child come up and look in the mirror). Who do you see? Notice it does not say dead *or* alive, but dead *and* alive (show the 'poster' to the rest of the children).

Do you know who wants us dead *and* alive? Not the sheriff but Jesus Christ. Jesus wants us to die to our old ways of living so that we can begin to live the way He wants us to: Dead to our old ways; alive to Jesus' ways.

I hope each one of you will decide to give yourself to Jesus if you haven't done so already. For Jesus is looking for you, and waiting to get you started in a wonderful new life with Him. —*Duane Kellogg*

Join the Fun

Now is the time of God's favor, now is the day of salvation.   —*2 Corinthians 6:2*

Objects Needed: Various kinds of invitations

Invitations are fun to receive. An invitation means that someone is having a party, a wedding, or a special dinner and they want you to be there. Not only do they want you to attend, but they want you to *participate*—join the fun and be part of the *celebration.*

The invitation will give all the information you need to know to attend—date, time, and place.

Sometimes at the bottom of an invitation will be the letters, R.S.V.P. Those letters mean that you should *respond* and let the host know whether you will be able to go to the celebration.

Parties are often planned to *honor* someone on their birthday, wedding, graduation, or retirement. When you accept an invitation you are honoring the guest of honor with your presence.

An invitation can be accepted or rejected. The choice is yours.

Usually when we say, "yes" to an invitation we enjoy the laughter, friendship, and special feeling of the celebration. We are glad we chose to go.

Have you ever thought about God's unique invitation? The Bible says that God is ready to welcome you right now. We have an open invitation to be part of the *celebration* of eternal life. Every day we can *participate* in His love.

The Bible, like an invitation, gives us all the information

we need to know to take part in the laughter, friendship, and special feeling of the celebration.

Our invitation from God has a R.S.V.P. The choice is ours and He wants us to *respond.*

When you accept God's invitation you are *honoring* Him.

An invitation offers us many possibilities. Take advantage of the joy that can be yours.

—*Lois Edstrom*

Born Again

I tell you the truth, unless a man is born again, he cannot see the kingdom of God.
—*John 3:3*

Objects Needed: Matches; a candle (have the candle lit before you begin)

I want all of you to pretend that this match is you. When you were born (strike the match) a new life came into the world. You and I were created by God and we were made to bring glory and honor to God.

But all of us, at some point in our lives—just like Adam, the very first person ever made—disobey God (blow match out). This is called sin. This sin separates us from God and we no longer are able to bring glory and honor to God no matter how hard we try.

The only way to get right with God again is through Jesus Christ. Our light must be renewed or restored. Jesus spoke of this as being born again. The only way this can be done is through Jesus Christ (relight match from candle). When we turn to Jesus in repentance and faith, we are born again and we can once again bring honor and glory to God. And that really is what life is all about.

—*Duane Kellogg*

41

Jesus is the Key

Whoever enters through me will be saved.
—*John 10:9*

Object Needed: A wooden box, or jewelry box, with a lock on it and some prize inside

I need a volunteer this morning; someone who's been good this past week and who would like to receive a little gift I have for them (choose a volunteer).

Okay, your gift is inside this box. All you have to do is open the box and reach in and take it and it's all yours. Go ahead. (Let the child fumble around with the lock for a moment.) What's the matter? Why don't you take the gift I have for you? Oh, the box is locked and you don't have the key! I'm sorry, I guess you can't have the gift. You'd better sit down (let the child turn to resume his seat).

Wait a minute! I have the key right here in my pocket. Now we can open the box and you can have your gift (open it up and let the child take the gift).

It's a good thing I had the key. Otherwise you wouldn't have received your present, no matter how good you were this week. When God gives us His gifts of forgiveness and love and faith, it is not because we deserve them for being good. You see, when we sinned and disobeyed God, it was like putting a lock on God's treasure chest of blessings for us. Once that lock was there, there was no way we could receive those blessings until the lock was unlocked. Do any of you know how the lock was unlocked so we can now receive God's gifts for us? It was unlocked by Jesus' death on the cross. By dying on the cross, Jesus removed the effects of our sin. His cross was like a key, unlocking the love and forgiveness and mercy of God for us.

If anyone wants to receive these things from God, they have to trust in Jesus and obey Him. Like a key He will unlock the treasure chest of God. God has some wonderful things for all of us, but we can only receive them because Jesus died for our sins.   —*Duane Kellogg*

STEWARDSHIP TALKS

Self-Denial

If anyone would come after me, he must deny himself and take up his cross and follow me.   —*Mark 8:34*

Object Needed: Sixteen quarters, in stacks of ten, five, and one

Self-denial means doing without something we need or want in order to give to others.

Let's pretend I'm on my way to the store to buy myself a candy bar, and I meet someone who is in great need of some money. I have ten quarters in my pocket, and I give him one of them. I still have nine quarters left, so I still can buy myself a candy bar that just costs one quarter. In fact, I can give him a quarter, buy myself the candy bar and still have eight quarters left in my pocket for myself. Giving such a small part of what I have left is not self-denial.

If I have these five quarters in my pocket and give one to someone who is in need, I can buy my candy bar and I would have three quarters in my pocket. Again, this would not be self-denial.

But if I have just one quarter with which to buy the candy bar and I give it to someone who needs it, I would have nothing left. That would be self-denial, because then I couldn't buy myself the candy bar.

That is what self-denial means—giving to someone when it means doing without something ourselves.

—*Idalee Vonk*

43

Gifts to Build the Church

There are different kinds of gifts, but the same Spirit. There are different kinds of service, but the same Lord.
— *1 Corinthians 12:4, 5*

Object Needed: A small box wrapped up like a gift, with a quarter inside

I need a volunteer this morning who would like to receive a gift (choose someone). Do you like to receive gifts? How many gifts do you have left from last Christmas that you haven't unwrapped yet?

When someone gives us a gift, we want to open up the package and see what is inside. If you never unwrap it, it won't do anyone any good at all.

Do you want to unwrap this gift? You may do so now, but there is one condition. You must agree to use this gift for the good of the church. Do you agree? (After child agrees, have him open the package.)

There, as you can see, I have given you a quarter. Since it is yours now, you can do whatever you want with it. You can buy a candy bar, you can save it, or you might want to put it in the offering plate this morning. It is up to you. But if you want to live up to our agreement, what do you think you will do with it?

When we become Christians, God gives us special gifts that are supposed to be used to build up the church. Unfortunately, many of us have never even bothered to open our gifts to see what they are, so they don't do anyone any good. Others of us are not using our gifts the way God intended. We are using them for selfish reasons rather than for the church.

God may have given you the gift of being able to encourage people, or to give generously, or to serve others in some way. Whatever gifts God has given you, remember to use them whenever you can to build up the church, for the church is precious to God.

—Duane Kellogg

Taking Care of Our Bodies

You are not your own; you were bought at a price. Therefore honor God with your body.
—1 Corinthians 6:19, 20

Objects needed: Two copies of the same magazine; one in good condition, the other having been mistreated and left outdoors all week.

Here are two magazines. Once they looked exactly alike. Both covers were bright and pretty. The inside pages of both magazines were smooth and clean. Now look at them. What a difference! And all because this one has been mistreated.

These magazines are like two men or two women who started out with strong, healthy, clean bodies—just as these magazines started out with clean, smooth pages. This man or woman took good care of his or her body (hold up good magazine). They formed good health habits when they were children. They ate the right foods, drank enough milk, played out in the fresh air and sunshine, and got plenty of sleep. As young people they continued following good health habits. They did not smoke or drink or use drugs.

This magazine that has been mistreated is like the people who mistreat their bodies. It is like men and women who started off on the wrong foot when they were children. They wanted to eat junk food instead of food that was good for them. They pouted each night when bedtime came because they wanted to stay up late. As young people they smoked and drank and started to use drugs. Soon they were not eating the right kinds of foods or getting enough rest. Their bodies became mistreated and looked like this mistreated magazine.

If you had to choose one of these magazines, which one would it be? Yes. This is the magazine you'd choose—the one that is clean and that has smooth pages and a bright picture on the cover. We don't even want to touch this magazine because it's so dirty and misused.

No one wants to read a dirty magazine. In the same way, no one wants to be near a man or woman who has ruined his body by not taking care of it. We are told to glorify God in our body and in our spirit. The only way we can do this is to take good care of our bodies when we are young, so we will grow into strong men and women with strong healthy bodies.

—*Idalee Vonk*

Sharing

Freely you have received, freely give.
—*Matthew 10:8*

Objects Needed: A lump of butter, a slice of bread, and a knife

Here we have a slice of bread and a lump of butter. There are several things we could do with this lump of butter. We could keep the butter in a lump in one corner of the slice, and eat all the butter at once. That would mean we would have to eat the rest of the slice of bread without butter.

(Spread half of the slice with the butter.) Or we could spread the butter over just half of the slice, but again we would have to eat some of the bread without butter.

(Spread the whole slice with butter.) Or we could spread the butter over the whole slice of bread. No part of the slice would be without butter, which means no part of the slice of bread would have to be eaten dry. So by spreading the butter over the entire slice of bread, we have made every bite taste good.

Sharing what we have with others is very much like spreading butter on a slice of bread. When we keep everything we have for ourselves and do not share with others, it's like eating the lump of butter in one bite. When we do that we have no butter left for the rest of the slice. When we keep everything for ourselves we become selfish and have nothing to give to others.

When we share just a little of what we have it's like spreading the butter over just half of the slice of bread. We have made a larger part of the slice taste good, but half of it is still dry. When we share just a little of what we have we make some people happy, but not as many as we could if we were more generous.

But when we are generous with everything we have and always share with others, it's like spreading the butter over the whole piece of bread. When we share generously with others, we spread as much happiness as possible.

And do you know the interesting thing about sharing? The more we share with others, the happier we make ourselves.

—*Idalee Vonk*

Use Money Wisely

Whoever sows sparingly will also reap sparingly, and whoever sows generously will also reap generously.

—2 Corinthians 9:6

Object Needed: A packet of seeds

Can you all see what I have in this packet? It's a bunch of seeds. Have any of you ever planted a seed and watched it grow into a plant? What would you think if someone did not have much food and was given a bag of seeds to plant, but instead just ate the seeds? That might make them feel better right at that moment, but what about later? If they had planted at least some of the seeds, then later they would have more food to eat and more seeds to plant. One little seed, depending on what it is, can produce a bush full of beans, or peas, or a plant loaded with tomatoes, or several ears of corn. If we eat the seed instead of planting it, we don't get very much out of it.

In a way money is like a seed. We can spend all the money we get on ourselves, which is like eating a seed, or we can give some of our money back to God, which is like planting a seed. God tells us in the Bible, that if we will remember to give a part of our money to Him, He will bless us and give us even more to use.

The next time you receive some money or earn some money, remember to set some of it aside for God. Just like a seed that is planted in the ground, that money will produce even more, which God will share with you.

—*Duane Kellogg*

48